ELEGANCE AND MENACE: WHAT JAMES BOND VILLAINS TEACH US

Chapter 1:

Villains Of Elegance And Menace

The James Bond franchise, born from the pen of Ian Fleming in 1953, has transcended its literary origins to become a global cinematic phenomenon. Fleming's creation, a suave secret agent with a penchant for danger, has captivated audiences for over seven decades. The character of James Bond, also known by his code number 007, became synonymous with espionage, sophistication, and thrilling adventure. But while Bond himself is the focal point of the series, the villains are integral to what makes the stories compelling.

Fleming's early Bond novels introduced readers to a range of adversaries who were as diverse in their malevolence as they were in their methods. From the enigmatic Dr. No to the megalomaniacal Goldfinger, these villains provided a mirror to Bond's own attributes and flaws. The antagonists were not just obstacles but essential elements that challenged Bond's ingenuity and moral compass, providing a framework within which his character could be tested and showcased.

As the franchise transitioned to the silver screen with "Dr. No" in 1962, the villains became even more central to the narrative. Sean Connery's Bond faced off against a series of larger-than-life adversaries who were often imbued with a blend of charm and menace. The villains of the early Bond films were not merely antagonists; they were often complex characters with elaborate schemes and personal vendettas, reflecting the Cold War anxieties and the socio-political climate of the time.

The Role of Villains in Bond Stories

The Bond villains serve a multifaceted role within the franchise. They are not just obstacles to be overcome but embodiments of larger themes and conflicts. Their significance can be explored through several key aspects:

The Antithesis of Bond

The most immediate role of the Bond villain is to serve as the antagonist to Bond's heroism. The villains often possess traits or ideologies that starkly contrast with Bond's values. For instance, while Bond embodies the ideals of loyalty, duty, and personal sacrifice, villains like Blofeld or Francisco Scaramanga often pursue self-serving agendas that threaten global stability.

In the 1964 film "Goldfinger," the villain Auric Goldfinger is driven by greed and a desire for ultimate wealth, his plan to irradiate the gold reserves at Fort Knox revealing his obsession with wealth and power. Bond's mission is to thwart Goldfinger's plan, underscoring the clash between personal greed and societal responsibility. This conflict highlights Bond's role as a protector of order and justice.

Representations of Contemporary Fears

Bond villains often embody contemporary fears and anxieties of the era. During the Cold War, villains like Dr. No and Rosa Klebb reflected the anxieties surrounding nuclear proliferation and espionage. In "You Only Live Twice," Blofeld's desire to instigate a global conflict mirrors the real-world tensions of the time.

In the post-Cold War era, the villains began to reflect new anxieties. The rise of terrorism, corporate corruption, and environmental destruction found their expressions in characters like Elliot Carver in "Tomorrow Never Dies" and Gustav Graves in "Die Another Day." These villains represent the shifting fears of a new global landscape, ensuring that Bond's adversaries remain relevant to contemporary issues.

The Personal Connection

A significant aspect of Bond villains is their personal connection to Bond. Many of Bond's adversaries have a history with him or share a personal vendetta. This personal connection adds depth to the conflict and often leads to a more intense and engaging narrative.

For example, in "Casino Royale" (2006), the antagonist Le Chiffre is a terrorist financier who directly challenges Bond's professional and personal resolve. The high-stakes poker game is not just a contest of skill but a battle of wits and willpower, with personal stakes that heighten the drama.

Similarly, in "Skyfall" (2012), the villain Raoul Silva has a personal grudge against MI6 and Bond himself. His background as a former agent with a deep-seated resentment towards the agency adds a layer of personal conflict that elevates the stakes of the story. Silva's vendetta is as much about revenge as it is about his ideology, creating a multi-dimensional antagonist who challenges Bond on both a professional and personal level.

The Ideological Challenge

Bond villains often present an ideological challenge that goes beyond mere criminal activity. Their schemes and motivations frequently reflect broader philosophical or political themes. This ideological dimension provides a framework for exploring complex questions of morality, power, and the nature of good and evil.

In "The Spy Who Loved Me" (1977), the villain Karl Stromberg is driven by a desire to create a new underwater civilization, reflecting a radical vision of a utopian society. His plan to destroy the surface world to build his underwater empire represents a fundamental challenge to the established order and Bond's own values. This ideological conflict adds depth to the narrative, transforming Bond's mission into a struggle over the future of humanity.

Similarly, in "No Time to Die" (2021), the villain Safin's plan to unleash a bioweapon reflects anxieties about bio-terrorism and the ethical implications of genetic manipulation. His motivations are driven by a complex mixture of revenge and a twisted vision of justice, presenting Bond with a challenge that goes beyond physical combat to encompass existential threats.

The Legacy of Bond Villains

The legacy of James Bond villains is not just in their immediate impact on the plots of the films and novels but in their lasting influence on popular culture. These characters have become archetypes in their own right, embodying various facets of villainy that continue to resonate with audiences.

The influence of Bond villains can be seen in the portrayal of antagonists in other media. The archetypal traits of Bond villains—such as their grandiose schemes, personal vendettas, and ideological motivations—have inspired a range of characters in films, television, and literature. The blend of charisma and menace that defines Bond villains has become a standard for crafting memorable and compelling antagonists.

Moreover, the Bond franchise has also evolved to reflect changing societal norms and values. The villains of today are more diverse and complex, often representing a range of global issues and ethical dilemmas. This evolution ensures that the franchise remains relevant and engaging, continuing to explore the nature of villainy in an ever-changing world.

Conclusion

The James Bond franchise has carved out a unique niche in the landscape of storytelling, thanks in no small part to its memorable and multifaceted villains. These antagonists are not merely obstacles but integral elements that define the narrative and thematic essence of the Bond stories. From their embodiment of contemporary fears to their personal connections with Bond, the villains of the franchise serve as crucial components in the ongoing exploration of morality, power, and justice.

As the franchise continues to evolve, the role of villains will undoubtedly remain central to its appeal. They challenge Bond in ways that go beyond physical confrontation, providing a mirror to his own values and actions. In this complex interplay between hero and villain, the James Bond franchise finds its enduring power, captivating audiences with tales of high-stakes adventure and timeless themes of good versus evil.

Chapter 2:

The Psychology Of Villainy In The James Bond Universe

The psychology of villainy in the James Bond universe is a fascinating exploration of the darker aspects of human nature. Bond villains often exhibit traits such as narcissism, megalomania, and psychopathy, which drive their nefarious schemes. These characters are typically motivated by a desire for power, wealth, or revenge, and their actions reflect a deep-seated need to assert control and dominance. The psychological complexity of these villains adds depth to their characters, making them more than just one-dimensional antagonists. By delving into their motivations and behaviors, the Bond films offer a compelling study of how personal traumas, societal pressures, and inherent personality disorders can shape individuals into formidable adversaries. This exploration not only enhances the narrative but also provides a mirror to the fears and anxieties of the audience, making the villains' eventual defeat all the more satisfying.

Understanding Motivations: Power, Revenge, Ideology

Power

Power is a central motif in the psychology of many Bond villains. It is not merely a desire for control but a fundamental drive that shapes their actions and schemes. For Ernst Stavro Blofeld, power is not just a means to an end but an end in itself. His overarching goal is to wield influence on a global scale, manipulating governments, organizations, and even the course of world events.

In "You Only Live Twice," Blofeld's plan to instigate a global conflict through the hijacking of spacecraft reflects a sophisticated strategy to manipulate international relations. His ambition is not merely to rule but to reshape the world order according to his vision. This drive for power is rooted in a profound need to assert dominance and control, which Blofeld achieves through a blend of charisma, intellect, and ruthlessness.

Psychologically, this quest for power can be traced to a desire for control and validation. Blofeld's actions illustrate how the need for power can become an all-consuming force, leading individuals to pursue increasingly extreme measures to maintain their dominance. This unrelenting ambition often blinds such characters to moral and ethical considerations, driving them to commit heinous acts in their pursuit of ultimate authority.

Revenge

Revenge is another powerful motivator for many Bond villains, providing a deeply personal drive that fuels their actions. Blofeld's quest for vengeance is intertwined with his desire for power, reflecting a complex interplay between personal grievances and broader ambitions.

In "Thunderball," Blofeld's vendetta against the world stems from his deep-seated resentment towards those he perceives as having wronged him. This personal grudge is coupled with a desire to enact retribution on a global scale. His revenge is not confined to individual targets but extends to the entire world, demonstrating how personal animosities can be amplified into grandiose schemes of destruction.

The psychology behind revenge is rooted in a sense of injustice and a desire for retribution. For Blofeld, the quest for revenge becomes a driving force that overrides rationality and humanity. This transformation illustrates how personal grievances can escalate into more dangerous and far-reaching consequences when combined with the desire for power.

Ideology

Ideology plays a crucial role in shaping the motivations of Bond villains. It provides a framework for understanding their actions and the justifications they use for their schemes. Blofeld's ideology, though often overshadowed by his desire for power and revenge, is a significant element of his character.

In "Diamonds Are Forever," Blofeld's ideological perspective is evident in his use of diamonds to finance his criminal activities. His actions reflect a worldview that values material wealth and technological advancement over human life and ethical considerations. Blofeld's ideology is marked by a belief in the superiority of his own vision for the world, leading him to pursue goals that disregard the well-being of others.

The psychological drive behind ideological motivations is often a combination of personal beliefs and a desire to impose those beliefs on others. For Blofeld, his ideology serves as a justification for his actions, allowing him to rationalize extreme measures as necessary for achieving his perceived goals. This blend of personal conviction and grandiosity underscores the dangers of unchecked ideological zeal.

Case Study: Ernst Stavro Blofeld as the Mastermind Archetype

Ernst Stavro Blofeld is one of the most iconic villains in the James Bond series, epitomizing the mastermind archetype. His character embodies the complexities of power, revenge, and ideology, making him an ideal case study for exploring the psychology of villainy.

Background and Development

Blofeld's background is marked by a blend of intelligence, ambition, and personal trauma. His character is defined by a profound sense of entitlement and a belief in his own superiority. The scar that disfigures his face symbolizes both his physical and emotional wounds, reflecting a past marked by betrayal and loss.

In Fleming's novels and the subsequent films, Blofeld's evolution from a shadowy figure to a central antagonist illustrates his growing ambition and influence. His plans are often grandiose and intricate, reflecting a strategic mind capable of manipulating global events. Blofeld's development from a peripheral character to the primary antagonist reveals the depth of his psychological complexity and the extent of his ambition.

Psychological Profile

From a psychological perspective, Blofeld exhibits traits associated with narcissism and megalomania. His need for power and control is coupled with a belief in his own superiority and a lack of empathy for others. This narcissistic personality is evident in his interactions with subordinates and his disregard for human life in pursuit of his goals.

Blofeld's megalomania is reflected in his elaborate schemes and grandiose plans. His belief in his own intellectual and strategic prowess drives him to undertake increasingly audacious and destructive actions. This sense of superiority often leads to a lack of foresight and an underestimation of his opponents, contributing to his eventual downfall.

Ambition and the Darker Sides of Human Nature

Blofeld's ambition serves as a lens through which the darker aspects of human nature are explored. His relentless pursuit of power and control reveals the potential for individuals to become consumed by their own desires, leading to destructive behavior and ethical lapses.

The psychology of ambition, as exemplified by Blofeld, highlights how the pursuit of power can lead to a disregard for moral considerations and a willingness to sacrifice others for personal gain. Blofeld's character serves as a cautionary tale about the dangers of unchecked ambition and the potential for individuals to lose sight of their humanity in the quest for dominance.

Lessons on Ambition

Blofeld's character provides valuable lessons on ambition and its consequences. His rise to power and subsequent downfall illustrate the dangers of allowing ambition to overshadow ethical considerations and the importance of maintaining a sense of responsibility and empathy.

The story of Blofeld underscores the need for individuals to balance their ambitions with an awareness of their impact on others. It serves as a reminder of the potential for ambition to become a destructive force when driven by unchecked desires and a lack of moral constraints.

Conclusion

The psychology of villainy in the James Bond universe provides a rich exploration of the motivations that drive individuals towards destructive behavior. Through the character of Ernst Stavro Blofeld, we gain insight into the complexities of power, revenge, and ideology, and the ways in which these motivations intersect to shape the actions of iconic villains.

Blofeld's role as the mastermind archetype highlights the interplay between personal grievances and grand ambitions, illustrating the darker sides of human nature and the consequences of unchecked ambition. His character serves as a powerful example of how psychological motivations can drive individuals to commit extreme acts in pursuit of their goals.

The lessons drawn from Blofeld's story offer valuable insights into the nature of ambition and the importance of maintaining ethical considerations in the pursuit of power. By understanding the psychological dynamics of villainy, we gain a deeper appreciation for the complexities of the James Bond universe and the enduring appeal of its iconic antagonists.

Chapter 3:

The Art Of Deception: The Mastery Of Villainy In James Bond Movies

Deception is a cornerstone of the James Bond villain archetype. In the intricate world of espionage and criminality depicted in Bond films, villains employ a range of deceptive tactics to achieve their goals. They use disguise, manipulation, and elaborate cons to outwit and outmaneuver their adversaries. This chapter delves into the art of deception as exemplified by two iconic villains: Dr. Kananga (alias Mr. Big) from *Live and Let Die* (1973) and Auric Goldfinger from *Goldfinger* (1964). Through their cunning use of disguise, manipulation, and the art of the con, these villains not only exemplify the seductive allure of deceit but also reveal the deeper consequences of their actions.

The Importance of Disguising Intentions and the Use of Emotional Manipulation

Disguising intentions and emotional manipulation are critical tools in the arsenal of a Bond villain. These tactics allow villains to conceal their true identities and intentions, gaining the upper hand over their adversaries. Disguise enables them to move undetected, infiltrate secure locations, and manipulate others without arousing suspicion. Manipulation, on the other hand, involves influencing and controlling others to achieve desired outcomes. This can be achieved through psychological tactics, exploitation of weaknesses, and strategic use of information.

The effectiveness of these methods lies in their ability to create a false sense of security and trust. By presenting a façade, villains can deceive their targets into believing they are harmless or even benevolent. This allows them to operate under the radar, orchestrating their schemes with minimal interference. The art of deception, therefore, is not just about hiding the truth but also about creating a convincing illusion that serves the villain's objectives.

Ways Bond Villains Use Deception and Manipulation to Gain What They Want

Bond villains employ a variety of deceptive and manipulative tactics to achieve their goals. These methods often involve a combination of disguise, psychological manipulation, and strategic deceit. Here are some common ways Bond villains use deception and manipulation:

Disguise and Dual Identities: Many Bond villains adopt alternate identities to conceal their true intentions. This allows them to operate in different spheres without drawing attention to their criminal activities.

Psychological Manipulation: Villains often exploit the fears, desires, and weaknesses of others to manipulate them. This can involve using threats, promises, or emotional appeals to control their targets.

Strategic Deceit: Bond villains frequently use misinformation and lies to mislead their adversaries. This can involve creating false narratives, planting misleading evidence, or using decoys to divert attention from their true plans.

Exploitation of Cultural Beliefs: Some villains use cultural or religious beliefs to manipulate others. This can involve exploiting superstitions, religious rituals, or traditional practices to instill fear and control.

Case Study: Dr. Kananga/Mr. Big in "Live and Let Die" Disguise and Dual Identity

Dr. Kananga, the dictator of the fictional Caribbean Island of San Monique, operates under the alias Mr. Big, a notorious drug lord in New York City. This dual identity allows him to conduct his illicit activities without drawing attention to his political position. As Mr. Big, Kananga controls a vast drug empire, using his legitimate diplomatic status to smuggle heroin into the United States. His ability to switch between these identities seamlessly is a testament to his mastery of disguise and deception.

Manipulation through Voodoo and Tarot

Kananga's manipulation extends beyond his dual identity. He employs Solitaire, a psychic medium and tarot card reader, to maintain control over his followers and instill fear in his enemies. Solitaire's predictions, combined with Kananga's use of voodoo rituals, create an aura of mysticism and supernatural power. This psychological manipulation ensures loyalty among his subordinates and deters potential threats. By exploiting cultural beliefs and superstitions, Kananga reinforces his authority and manipulates those around him to serve his interests.

Consequences of Deceit

Kananga's elaborate web of deceit ultimately leads to his downfall. His reliance on disguise and manipulation creates vulnerabilities that Bond exploits. When Bond uncovers Kananga's true identity and exposes his drug operation, the carefully constructed façade crumbles. The consequences of Kananga's deceit are severe, resulting in his death and the dismantling of his criminal empire. This case study illustrates the inherent risks of deception; while it can provide short-term advantages, it also creates opportunities for exposure and retribution.

Case Study: Auric Goldfinger in "Goldfinger"
Greed and the Art of the Con

Auric Goldfinger is driven by an insatiable greed for gold, which he pursues through elaborate cons and schemes. His obsession with the precious metal leads him to devise Operation Grand Slam, a plan to irradiate the United States' gold reserves at Fort Knox, thereby increasing the value of his own gold stockpile. Goldfinger's ability to present himself as a legitimate businessman while secretly orchestrating criminal activities exemplifies the art of the con.

Smuggling Gold under Legitimate Guise

Goldfinger's smuggling operations are a key aspect of his deception. He uses his legitimate business, Auric Enterprises, as a front to transport gold across borders. By disguising gold bars as components of his Rolls Royce and using his smelting facilities to refine and rebrand the gold, Goldfinger evades detection and maximizes his profits. This method of smuggling highlights the effectiveness of blending legitimate operations with illicit activities, making it difficult for authorities to uncover the truth.

Consequences of Deceit

Goldfinger's deceitful practices ultimately lead to his undoing. Bond's investigation exposes the true nature of Goldfinger's operations, culminating in a dramatic confrontation at Fort Knox. The consequences of Goldfinger's greed and deception are catastrophic, resulting in his death and the failure of his grand scheme. This case study underscores the destructive power of unchecked ambition and the inevitable downfall that accompanies deceit.

Methods People Use Today to Deceive and Manipulate Us

Deception and manipulation are not confined to the world of James Bond; they are prevalent in everyday life. Here are some common methods people use today to deceive and manipulate others:

Emotional Manipulation: Manipulators often exploit emotions such as fear, guilt, and sympathy to control others. This can involve playing the victim, using flattery, or creating a sense of urgency to influence decisions.

Misinformation and Lies: Deceivers frequently spread false information or distort the truth to mislead others. This can involve exaggerating facts, omitting crucial details, or fabricating stories to create a desired narrative.

Psychological Tactics: Manipulators use various psychological tactics to confuse and control their targets. This can include gaslighting, guilt-tripping, and playing mind games to undermine confidence and create dependency.

Exploitation of Trust: Deceivers often build trust and rapport with their targets before exploiting that trust for personal gain. This can involve pretending to be a friend, offering help, or providing false assurances to gain influence.

How We Can Use What We Learn from Bond Villains to Thwart Those Who Wish to Deceive and Manipulate Us

The lessons we learn from Bond villains can be invaluable in recognizing and thwarting deception and manipulation in our own lives. Here are some strategies to protect ourselves:

Stay Informed and Skeptical: Knowledge is power. Stay informed about common manipulation tactics and be skeptical of information that seems too good to be true. Verify facts and seek multiple sources before making decisions.

Set Boundaries: Establish clear boundaries and be assertive in maintaining them. Manipulators often exploit weak boundaries, so it's important to communicate your limits and stand firm against attempts to cross them.

Trust Your Instincts: Pay attention to your gut feelings. If something feels off or too good to be true, it probably is. Trust your instincts and investigate further before committing to anything.

Seek Support: Don't hesitate to seek support from trusted friends, family, or professionals if you suspect manipulation. They can provide valuable perspectives and help you navigate complex situations.

Educate Yourself on Emotional Intelligence: Understanding your own emotions and those of others can help you recognize manipulation attempts. Emotional intelligence can empower you to respond effectively and maintain control over your decisions.

Conclusion

The art of deception is a central theme in the James Bond franchise, with villains employing disguise, manipulation, and cunning to achieve their goals. The case studies of Dr. Kananga and Auric Goldfinger illustrate the effectiveness and risks of these tactics. While deception can provide significant advantages, it also creates vulnerabilities that can be exploited by adversaries. The consequences of deceit are often severe, leading to the downfall of even the most cunning villains. By examining these characters and their methods, we gain valuable insights into the complexities of human behavior and the precarious nature of deception. These lessons can help us recognize and thwart manipulation in our own lives, empowering us to navigate a world where deception is an ever-present threat.

Chapter 4:

The Dark Side Of Innovation: How James Bond Villains Manipulate Technology For Evil

The dark side of innovation is vividly portrayed through the actions of James Bond villains, who often manipulate cutting-edge technology for nefarious purposes. These antagonists harness technological advancements to execute grandiose schemes, ranging from global surveillance to cyberterrorism. For instance, Raoul Silva in "Skyfall" uses his hacking skills to wreak havoc on MI6, demonstrating the destructive potential of cyber warfare. Similarly, Elliot Carver in "Tomorrow Never Dies" exploits media technology to incite international conflict for personal gain. These villains' actions highlight the ethical dilemmas and potential dangers associated with technological progress, serving as a cautionary tale about the misuse of innovation. By showcasing the malevolent use of technology, the Bond films underscore the importance of ethical considerations and the need for vigilance in the face of rapid technological advancements. The digital age has ushered in unprecedented advances in technology and innovation, reshaping the way we live, work, and interact. In the James Bond universe, villains like Elliot Carver and Raoul Silva embody the darker side of these advancements, using technology to further their nefarious agendas. This chapter explores how Bond villains exploit technology for evil purposes, with a focus on cyberterrorism and the implications of digital innovation. Through case studies of Carver and Silva, we'll examine the strategies employed to manipulate technology and the ethical lessons they impart.

Technology as a Tool for Villainy

1. Exploiting Technological Advancements
In the digital age, technology has become a double-edged

sword, offering both incredible benefits and significant risks. For James Bond villains, technological advancements present opportunities to gain an advantage and execute elaborate plans. Carver and Silva are prime examples of how technology can be weaponized to achieve malevolent objectives.

Elliot Carver's scheme in *Tomorrow Never Dies* (1997) revolves around his media empire, which serves as a front for his true ambitions. Carver's control over global news networks allows him to manipulate information and create a fabricated reality. By using satellite technology and advanced media systems, Carver orchestrates a series of events designed to incite global conflict. His ability to control the news and manipulate public perception demonstrates how technology can be wielded to influence political and social outcomes.

Raoul Silva, from *Skyfall* (2012), employs a different approach. As a former MI6 agent turned cyberterrorist, Silva utilizes advanced hacking techniques to infiltrate and dismantle critical infrastructure. His cyber-attacks on MI6's systems and the broader digital landscape reveal the vulnerabilities inherent in modern technology. Silva's ability to exploit digital networks and compromise sensitive information underscores the potential for technology to be used as a tool for widespread disruption and chaos.

2. Cyberterrorism: The New Frontier of Villainy

Cyberterrorism represents a contemporary and increasingly potent form of villainy. The digital realm offers a new battleground for conflicts, with cyber-attacks capable of causing significant damage to infrastructure, economies, and national security. Carver and Silva exemplify how cyberterrorism can be used to further villainous objectives, leveraging technology to inflict harm on a global scale.

Elliot Carver: The Power of Media Manipulation

Elliot Carver's primary weapon is his media empire, which he uses to manipulate public perception and incite conflict. Carver's technological prowess is evident in his control over satellite communications and digital news platforms. By broadcasting false information and creating fabricated news stories, he engineers crises and manipulates public opinion.

Carver's plan to incite a war between the UK and China is a prime example of how technology can be used to exploit geopolitical tensions. His manipulation of media coverage and news reports creates a fabricated narrative that escalates conflicts and drives nations toward confrontation. Carver's scheme highlights the power of media and technology in shaping perceptions and influencing political outcomes.

Raoul Silva: The Threat of Digital Infiltration

Raoul Silva's approach to cyberterrorism is characterized by his sophisticated hacking skills and his ability to compromise digital systems. Silva's attacks on MI6 and other targets reveal the vulnerabilities of modern technology and the potential for digital threats to disrupt national security.

Silva's infiltration of MI6's computer systems allow him to access classified information and manipulate internal operations. His ability to launch cyber-attacks and compromise sensitive data demonstrates the risks associated with digital innovation. Silva's actions illustrate how technology can be weaponized to target critical infrastructure and disrupt global stability.

Case Studies: Technology and Innovation in Action

1. Elliot Carver: Media Mogul and Manipulator
Technological Strategies:

Elliot Carver's use of technology is both sophisticated and insidious. His media empire, encompassing television networks, newspapers, and digital platforms, serves as a vehicle for his grand scheme. Carver's control over satellite technology enables him to broadcast manipulated news reports and create false narratives.

Carver's technological strategy includes:

- **Satellite Control:** Carver's access to satellite communications allows him to transmit fabricated news reports and manipulate global media coverage. By controlling the flow of information, he engineers crises and shapes public perception.
- **News Manipulation:** Carver's ability to create and disseminate false news stories generates fear and conflict. His manipulation of media narratives drives international tensions and fuels his plan to instigate a war.

Ethical Implications:

Carver's use of technology raises important ethical questions about the role of media and information in society. His actions highlight the potential for technology to be misused for manipulative purposes, emphasizing the need for ethical standards in media and communication. The ability to shape public perception and influence political outcomes through technology underscores the importance of responsible and transparent information dissemination.

2. Raoul Silva: The Cyberterrorist

Technological Strategies:

Raoul Silva's cyberterrorism is characterized by his expertise in hacking and digital infiltration. His attacks on MI6 and other targets reveal the vulnerabilities of modern technology and the potential for digital threats to cause widespread disruption.

Silva's technological strategy includes:

- **Hacking and Infiltration:** Silva's ability to compromise MI6's computer systems allow him to access classified information and manipulate internal operations. His hacking skills enable him to launch sophisticated cyber-attacks and disrupt critical infrastructure.

- **Digital Warfare:** Silva's cyber-attacks are designed to create chaos and undermine national security. His ability to launch coordinated attacks on digital networks highlights the risks associated with digital innovation and the potential for technology to be used as a tool for destruction.

Ethical Implications:

Silva's use of technology raises significant ethical concerns about cybersecurity and digital warfare. His actions highlight the potential for technology to be weaponized and used to compromise national security and disrupt critical infrastructure. The ethical implications of cyberterrorism emphasize the need for robust cybersecurity measures and ethical considerations in the development and use of digital technologies.

Lessons on the Ethical Implications of Technology and Innovation

1. The Power of Information

The manipulation of information is a powerful tool that can shape public perception and influence political outcomes. Carver's use of media technology to create false narratives and incite conflict underscores the impact that information can have on society. The ethical lesson here is the importance of responsible information dissemination and the need for transparency and accuracy in media reporting.

2. The Vulnerability of Digital Systems

The exploitation of digital systems and the vulnerabilities associated with cybersecurity are central to Silva's scheme. His ability to infiltrate and compromise critical infrastructure highlights the risks inherent in digital innovation. The ethical lesson is the need for robust cybersecurity measures and the importance of safeguarding sensitive information to prevent malicious attacks.

3. The Consequences of Technological Misuse

Both Carver and Silva illustrate the potential consequences of technological misuse. Carver's manipulation of media leads to global conflict, while Silva's cyber-attacks disrupt national security. The ethical lesson is the responsibility of individuals and organizations to use technology for positive purposes and to consider the potential consequences of their actions.

4. The Need for Ethical Standards in Technology

The actions of Carver and Silva emphasize the need for ethical standards in the development and use of technology. The potential for technology to be misused for malicious purposes underscores the importance of ethical considerations in technological innovation. Responsible development and use of technology are essential to prevent exploitation and harm.

Conclusion

The manipulation of technology by James Bond villains like Elliot Carver and Raoul Silva provides a compelling exploration of the dark side of innovation. Their use of technology to further their nefarious agendas highlights the potential for technological advancements to be weaponized and exploited for evil purposes. Through their schemes, we gain insight into the ethical implications of technology and the importance of responsible innovation.

Carver's control over media technology and Silva's cyberterrorism demonstrates how technology can be used to influence public perception, compromise national security, and cause widespread disruption. The lessons drawn from their actions emphasize the need for ethical standards, robust cybersecurity measures, and responsible use of technology to prevent exploitation and harm.

As we continue to advance in the digital age, the lessons from Bond villains serve as a reminder of the potential risks and ethical considerations associated with technological innovation.

By understanding the dark side of technology and innovation, we can better navigate the challenges and opportunities of the digital era, ensuring that technology is used for positive purposes and the greater good.

Chapter 5:

The Power Of Charisma Of Villains In The James Bond Movies

The James Bond franchise is renowned for its suave protagonist, thrilling action sequences, and, notably, its charismatic villains. These antagonists are not merely evil for the sake of being evil; they possess a magnetic charm that captivates audiences and makes their villainy all the more compelling. This a-chapter delves into the allure of charm and persuasion in Bond villains, with a focus on Francisco Scaramanga from "The Man with the Golden Gun" and Le Chiffre from "Casino Royale." Through these case studies, we will explore the lessons on influence, persuasion, and the inherent risks of charm.

The Allure of Charm and Persuasion

Charisma is a powerful tool in the arsenal of any villain. It allows them to manipulate, deceive, and control others with ease. In the world of James Bond, where the stakes are always high, the ability to charm and persuade is often what sets the most memorable villains apart. These characters use their charisma to gain the trust of others, mask their true intentions, and ultimately achieve their nefarious goals.

Case Study: Francisco Scaramanga in "The Man with the Golden Gun"

Francisco Scaramanga, portrayed by Christopher Lee, is one of the most charismatic villains in the Bond franchise. Known as "The Man with the Golden Gun," Scaramanga is a skilled assassin who charges a million dollars per hit. His charm and sophistication are evident in his interactions with Bond and others, making him a formidable adversary.

Dueling with Fate and Charisma

Scaramanga's charisma is most evident in his ability to manipulate those around him. He exudes confidence and charm, which he uses to disarm his opponents and lure them into a false sense of security. This is particularly evident in his interactions with Bond, where he engages in a psychological game of cat and mouse. Scaramanga's charm is not just a superficial trait; it is a strategic tool that he uses to gain the upper hand.

One of the most iconic scenes in the film is the duel between Bond and Scaramanga. The setting, a secluded island with a funhouse-like arena, is a testament to Scaramanga's flair for the dramatic. His charisma is on full display as he taunts Bond, using his charm to unsettle and distract him. This scene highlights the power of charisma in creating tension and suspense, making Scaramanga a memorable and captivating villain.

Lessons on Influence and Persuasion

Scaramanga's character teaches us several lessons about influence and persuasion:

1. Confidence is Key: Scaramanga's unwavering confidence in his abilities makes him a formidable opponent. Confidence can be a powerful tool in persuasion, as it can inspire trust and admiration in others.
2. Charm as a Weapon: Scaramanga uses his charm to manipulate and control those around him. This highlights the importance of charisma in gaining influence and achieving one's goals.
3. Psychological Manipulation: Scaramanga's ability to play mind games with Bond demonstrates the power of psychological manipulation. Understanding the psychology of others can be a crucial aspect of persuasion.

Case Study: Le Chiffre In "Casino Royale"

Le Chiffre, portrayed by Mads Mikkelsen, is another iconic Bond villain known for his charisma and cunning. As a financier for terrorist organizations, Le Chiffre is a master of deception and manipulation. His charm and intelligence make him a dangerous adversary for Bond.

Gambling with Fate and Charisma

Le Chiffre's charisma is most evident in the high-stakes poker game at the Casino Royale. This game is not just a test of skill but also a battle of wits and psychological endurance. Le Chiffre's calm demeanor and strategic thinking make him a formidable opponent at the poker table. His ability to read his opponents and manipulate the game in his favor is a testament to his charisma and intelligence.

One of the most memorable scenes in the film is the intense poker showdown between Bond and Le Chiffre. Throughout the game, Le Chiffre uses his charm and psychological tactics to unsettle Bond and gain the upper hand. His ability to remain composed under pressure and his strategic use of charm make him a captivating and formidable villain.

Lessons on Influence and Persuasion

Le Chiffre's character provides valuable lessons on influence and persuasion:

1. Strategic Thinking: Le Chiffre's success at the poker table is a result of his strategic thinking and ability to read his opponents. This highlights the importance of strategy and intelligence in persuasion.

2. Composure Under Pressure: Le Chiffre's ability to remain calm and composed under pressure is a key aspect of his charisma. Maintaining composure in high-stakes situations can enhance one's influence and effectiveness.

3. Psychological Tactics: Le Chiffre's use of psychological tactics to manipulate his opponents demonstrates the power of understanding and exploiting the psychology of others.

The Risks of Charm

While charisma can be a powerful tool, it also comes with inherent risks. The very traits that make charismatic villains so compelling can also lead to their downfall. Overconfidence, manipulation, and deceit can create enemies and lead to a loss of trust and credibility.

In the case of Francisco Scaramanga, his overconfidence ultimately leads to his demise. His belief in his own invincibility blinds him to the possibility of defeat, allowing Bond to outsmart him in the final duel. Similarly, Le Chiffre's reliance on manipulation and deceit ultimately leads to his downfall. His failure to anticipate Bond's resilience and resourcefulness results in his defeat at the poker table and his eventual demise.

These examples highlight the double-edged nature of charisma. While it can be a powerful tool for influence and persuasion, it can also lead to overconfidence and a lack of foresight. Understanding the risks of charm is crucial for anyone seeking to wield it effectively.

Conclusion

The power of charisma in James Bond villains is a testament to the allure of charm and persuasion. Characters like Francisco Scaramanga and Le Chiffre use their charisma to manipulate, deceive, and control those around them, creating compelling and memorable antagonists. Through their stories, we learn valuable lessons about influence, persuasion, and the risks of charm. In the high-stakes world of James Bond, charisma is both a weapon and a vulnerability, making it a fascinating and complex aspect of villainy.

Chapter 6:

Three Moves Ahead: The Implications Of Strategy For Bond Villains

In the world of James Bond, villains are not just adversaries; they are masterminds whose intricate plans and strategic foresight create the high-stakes scenarios that define the franchise. This article explores the implications of strategy for Bond villains, focusing on the meticulous planning and foresight that underpin their villainous plots. Through case studies of Emilio Largo from "Thunderball" and Dominic Greene from "Quantum of Solace," we will examine how these characters exemplify long-term strategic thinking and patience in both business and crime.

Planning and Foresight in Villainous Plots

The success of a Bond villain often hinges on their ability to plan meticulously and anticipate potential obstacles. This strategic foresight allows them to execute complex schemes that challenge James Bond and create compelling narratives. Villains like Emilio Largo and Dominic Greene demonstrate how careful planning and long-term thinking are essential components of their villainy.

Case Study: Emilio Largo in "Thunderball"

Emilio Largo, portrayed by Adolfo Celi, is a prime example of a Bond villain whose strategic planning and foresight are central to his character. As the second-in-command of the criminal organization SPECTRE, Largo is tasked with executing Operation Thunderball, a plan to hijack NATO nuclear warheads and hold the world to ransom.

The Role of Angelo Palazzi

One of the key elements of Largo's plan involves Angelo Palazzi, a SPECTRE operative who undergoes plastic surgery to assume the identity of NATO pilot François Derval. This elaborate ruse requires extensive planning and coordination, highlighting Largo's strategic acumen.

1. **Recruitment and Preparation**: Largo recruits Palazzi and oversees his transformation into Derval. This process involves not only plastic surgery but vocal training and behavioral conditioning to ensure Palazzi can convincingly impersonate the NATO pilot.
2. **Execution of the Plan**: On the day of the NATO exercise, Palazzi successfully infiltrates the airbase and takes control of the plane carrying the nuclear warheads.
3. **Betrayal and Elimination**: Despite Palazzi's successful execution of the plan, Largo betrays him. When Palazzi demands more money for his efforts, Largo personally ensures his demise by severing his oxygen supply, leaving him to drown. This ruthless act underscores Largo's willingness to eliminate any potential threats to his plan.

Strategic Implications

Largo's use of Palazzi demonstrates several key aspects of strategic planning:

- **Attention to Detail**: Largo's plan involves meticulous attention to detail, from the physical transformation of Palazzi to the precise timing of the hijacking. This level of detail is crucial for the success of complex schemes.
- **Contingency Planning**: By eliminating Palazzi, Largo removes a potential liability. This act of betrayal highlights the importance of contingency planning and the willingness to take decisive action to protect the overall strategy.
- **Long-Term Thinking**: Largo's plan is not just about immediate gains but also about maintaining SPECTRE's position of power. His strategic foresight ensures that the organization can continue to operate without

exposure or interference.

Case Study: Dominic Greene in "Quantum of Solace"

Dominic Greene, portrayed by Mathieu Amalric, is another Bond villain whose strategic thinking and long-term planning are central to his character. As the head of the environmentalist organization Greene Planet, Greene uses his position to manipulate global resources for the benefit of the criminal organization Quantum.

The Eco-Friendly Facade

Greene's plan involves setting up an eco-friendly company, Greene Planet, as a front for his true intentions. This facade allows him to operate under the guise of environmentalism while pursuing his nefarious goals.

1. **Establishing Greene Planet**: Greene establishes Greene Planet as a legitimate environmental organization, buying up large tracts of land for ecological preservation. This provides him with a cover for his activities and allows him to gain the trust of governments and international organizations.

2. **Manipulating the Water Supply**: Greene's ultimate goal is to control Bolivia's water supply. He orchestrates a coup to install a puppet government that will grant him control over the country's water resources. By creating artificial water shortages, Greene plans to sell water at exorbitant prices, thereby gaining immense power and wealth.

3. **Deception and Manipulation**: Throughout the film, Greene uses his charm and persuasive skills to manipulate those around him. He deceives both allies and enemies, maintaining his façade of environmentalism while pursuing his true objectives.

Strategic Implications

Greene's actions highlight several important aspects of

strategic planning:

- **Long-Term Vision**: Greene's plan to control Bolivia's water supply is a long-term strategy that requires patience and careful execution. This vision allows him to pursue his goals methodically, without drawing undue attention.
- **Use of Deception**: Greene's ability to maintain his eco-friendly facade while manipulating global resources demonstrates the power of deception in strategic planning. By presenting himself as a benevolent environmentalist, he is able to operate without suspicion.
- **Leveraging Resources**: Greene's control over Greene Planet allows him to leverage significant resources for his plan. This highlights the importance of resource management in executing complex strategies.

Lessons on Strategic Thinking and Patience

The cases of Emilio Largo and Dominic Greene provide valuable lessons on the importance of strategic thinking and patience in both business and crime. These villains demonstrate how careful planning, attention to detail, and long-term vision are essential components of successful schemes.

1. **Meticulous Planning**: Both Largo and Greene invest significant time and effort into planning their schemes. This meticulous planning ensures that they can anticipate potential obstacles and respond effectively.
2. **Contingency Planning**: The ability to adapt and respond to changing circumstances is crucial for strategic success. Both villains demonstrate the importance of having contingency plans in place to address unforeseen challenges.
3. **Long-Term Vision**: Successful strategies often require a long-term perspective. Largo and Greene both pursue

goals that extend beyond immediate gains, focusing on maintaining power and influence over time.

4. **Deception and Manipulation**: The use of deception and manipulation is a common theme in the strategies of both villains. By presenting false fronts and misleading their adversaries, they are able to achieve their objectives without detection.

5. **Patience and Persistence**: Strategic success often requires patience and persistence. Both Largo and Greene demonstrate the importance of staying committed to their plans, even in the face of setbacks and challenges.

Conclusion

The implications of strategy for Bond villains are profound, shaping the narratives and conflicts that define the franchise. Through the meticulous planning and foresight of characters like Emilio Largo and Dominic Greene, we see how strategic thinking and patience are essential components of villainy. These villains provide valuable lessons on the importance of long-term vision, attention to detail, and the power of deception in achieving one's goals. In the high-stakes world of James Bond, the ability to think strategically and act decisively is what sets the most memorable villains apart.

Chapter 7:

The Feminine Touch: The Intriguing World Of Female Villains In James Bond Movies

The James Bond franchise is renowned for its iconic villains, who often serve as the perfect foils to the suave and sophisticated. While male villains like Ernst Stavro Blofeld and Goldfinger have left an indelible mark on the series, the female villains bring a unique blend of charm, cunning, and complexity. We explore the distinct characteristics of female Bond villains, focusing on Rosa Klebb from "From Russia with Love," Fiona Volpe from "Thunderball," Elektra King from "The World is Not Enough," and Vesper Lynd from "Casino Royale." Through these case studies, we will examine the strong female archetypes they portray, the complexity of their situations, and the lessons we can learn from their stories.

The Difference Between Male and Female Bond Villains

Male Bond villains are often characterized by their grandiose schemes, physical prowess, and a desire for world domination. They are typically portrayed as larger-than-life figures with a clear-cut evil agenda. In contrast, female Bond villains often exhibit a more nuanced approach to villainy. They rely on their intelligence, charm, and manipulation to achieve their goals. Their motivations are often more personal and complex, adding depth to their characters and making them intriguing adversaries for James Bond.

Case Study: Rosa Klebb in "From Russia with Love"

Rosa Klebb, portrayed by Lotte Lenya, is one of the most memorable female villains in the Bond franchise. As a high-ranking member of the criminal organization SPECTRE, Klebb is a formidable adversary who uses her intelligence and ruthlessness to further her organization's goals.

Klebb is a strong female archetype, embodying traits such as determination, intelligence, and authority. She is not merely a henchwoman but a key player in SPECTRE's operations. Her role as a former Soviet counter-intelligence operative turned SPECTRE agent highlights her strategic mind and ability to navigate complex political landscapes.

Klebb's situation is complex, as she must balance her loyalty to SPECTRE with her personal ambitions. Her defection from the Soviet Union to SPECTRE adds an additional layer of intrigue to her character. She is tasked with orchestrating a plot to steal a Lektor decoding machine and eliminate James Bond, showcasing her ability to plan and execute intricate schemes.

From Rosa Klebb, we learn the importance of strategic thinking and adaptability. Her ability to switch allegiances and navigate different power structures demonstrates the value of flexibility in achieving one's goals. Additionally, her ruthless approach to eliminating threats highlights the potential dangers of unchecked ambition and the ethical considerations that come with it.

Case Study: Fiona Volpe in "Thunderball"

Fiona Volpe, portrayed by Luciana Paluzzi, is another iconic female villain in the Bond series. As an agent of SPECTRE, Volpe is known for her seductive charm and lethal skills, making her a formidable opponent for James Bond.

Volpe embodies the femme fatale archetype, using her beauty and charm to manipulate those around her. She is confident, assertive, and unafraid to use her sexuality as a weapon. Her ability to seduce and deceive highlights her intelligence and strategic mind.

Volpe's situation is complex, as she must navigate the dangerous world of espionage while maintaining her cover. Her loyalty to SPECTRE and her willingness to carry out dangerous missions demonstrate her commitment to her cause. However, her interactions with Bond reveal a deeper complexity, as she must balance her professional duties with her personal desires.

From Fiona Volpe, we learn the power of charm and persuasion. Her ability to manipulate others through her charisma highlights the importance of interpersonal skills in achieving one's objectives. Additionally, her willingness to take risks and embrace danger demonstrates the value of courage and determination in the face of adversity.

Case Study: Elektra King in "The World is Not Enough"

Elektra King, portrayed by Sophie Marceau, is a unique and complex villain in the Bond franchise. As an oil heiress with a tragic past, King uses her intelligence and charm to manipulate those around her and further her own agenda.

King is a strong female archetype, embodying traits such as resilience, intelligence, and ambition. Her ability to navigate the male-dominated world of the oil industry and execute her plans demonstrates her strength and determination.

King's situation is deeply complex, as she is both a victim and a villain. Her kidnapping and subsequent manipulation by Renard, another antagonist in the film, add layers to her character. Her desire for revenge and control over her own destiny drive her actions, making her a multifaceted and intriguing villain.

From Elektra King, we learn the importance of resilience and the power of personal agency. Her ability to overcome her traumatic past and take control of her future highlights the value of inner strength and determination. Additionally, her willingness to manipulate and deceive others for her own gain serves as a cautionary tale about the ethical implications of ambition and the potential consequences of unchecked power.

Case Study: Vesper Lynd in "Casino Royale"

Vesper Lynd, portrayed by Eva Green, is a complex and tragic character in the Bond franchise. As a British Treasury agent who becomes romantically involved with James Bond, Lynd's actions and motivations are deeply intertwined with her personal and professional life.

Lynd embodies the strong female archetype through her intelligence, independence, and emotional depth. Her ability to hold her own in a male-dominated world and her complex relationship with Bond highlight her strength and resilience.

Lynd's situation is highly complex, as she is caught between her duty to her country and her love for Bond. Her involvement with the criminal organization Quantum and her ultimate betrayal of Bond adds layers to her character. Her actions are driven by a desire to protect someone she loves, making her a sympathetic and tragic figure.

From Vesper Lynd, we learn the importance of emotional intelligence and the complexities of human relationships. Her ability to navigate her conflicting loyalties and emotions highlights the value of empathy and understanding. Additionally, her tragic fate serves as a reminder of the potential consequences of deception and the importance of honesty and integrity in personal and professional relationships.

The Strong Female Archetype

The female villains in the James Bond franchise often portray strong female archetypes. They are intelligent, resourceful, and assertive, using their skills and charm to achieve their goals. Unlike their male counterparts, who often rely on brute force and grandiose schemes, these women use their wits and interpersonal skills to manipulate and control those around them. This portrayal of strong female characters adds depth and complexity to the Bond series, making these villains memorable and compelling.

The Complexity of Their Situations

The situations that female Bond villains find themselves in are often more complex than those of their male counterparts. They must navigate a world dominated by men, using their intelligence and charm to achieve their goals. Their motivations are often deeply personal, driven by a desire for revenge, power, or control. This complexity adds layers to their characters, making them more relatable and intriguing. Whether it's Rosa Klebb's defection to SPECTRE, Fiona Volpe's balancing act between professional duties and personal desires, Elektra King's quest for revenge, or Vesper Lynd's conflicting loyalties, these female villains face multifaceted challenges that shape their actions and decisions.

Moral Lessons We Can Learn

The stories of female Bond villains offer several moral lessons. Firstly, they highlight the importance of strategic thinking and adaptability. Characters like Rosa Klebb and Elektra King demonstrate the value of being able to navigate complex power structures and switch allegiances when necessary. Secondly, they underscore the power of charm and persuasion. Fiona Volpe's ability to manipulate others through her charisma shows the importance of interpersonal skills in achieving one's objectives. Lastly, they serve as cautionary tales about the ethical implications of ambition and the potential consequences of deception. Vesper Lynd's tragic fate reminds us of the importance of honesty and integrity in personal and professional relationships.

The Changing Image of Women as Powerful Leaders

The portrayal of female villains in the James Bond franchise reflects the changing image of women as powerful leaders. These characters are not just sidekicks or love interests; they are formidable adversaries who use their intelligence, charm, and resilience to achieve their goals. This shift in portrayal mirrors broader societal changes, where women are increasingly recognized for their leadership abilities and contributions. As the Bond franchise continues to evolve, we can expect to see more complex and powerful female villains who challenge traditional gender roles and bring new dimensions to the series.

Conclusion

The female villains in the James Bond franchise bring a unique blend of charm, intelligence, and complexity to the series. Characters like Rosa Klebb, Fiona Volpe, Elektra King, and Vesper Lynd showcase the diverse ways in which women can embody villainy, using their strengths and navigating complex situations to achieve their goals. Through their stories, we learn valuable lessons about strategic thinking, resilience, charm, and the ethical implications of ambition. These strong female archetypes add depth and intrigue to the Bond franchise, making them unforgettable adversaries for 007.

Chapter 8:

The Role Of Loyalty And Betrayal: The Relationships Between James Bond Villains And Their Henchmen

In the James Bond franchise, the villains are often accompanied by henchmen who play crucial roles in executing their nefarious plans. These henchmen are not just mere sidekicks; they are formidable adversaries in their own right, each with unique skills and characteristics that make them memorable. This article explores the role of henchmen in the Bond movies, focusing on the themes of loyalty and betrayal in their relationships with the villains. Through case studies of Oddjob, Jaws, Nick Nack, and Mr. Hinx, we will examine how these characters define the archetype of the henchman and the dynamics of their loyalty to their masters.

The Role of Henchmen in James Bond Movies

Henchmen in James Bond movies serve several key functions. They are the enforcers, carrying out the physical and often brutal tasks that the main villains delegate. They provide a direct threat to Bond, engaging him in combat and creating obstacles that he must overcome. Henchmen also add depth to the villains' characters, highlighting their power and influence by showcasing the loyalty and fear they command. These characters often possess unique traits or abilities that make them stand out, contributing to the iconic status of the Bond franchise.

Case Study: Oddjob: The Original Henchman

Oddjob, portrayed by Harold Sakata, is one of the most iconic henchmen in the Bond series. Appearing in "Goldfinger," Oddjob is the loyal servant of Auric Goldfinger, known for his lethal hat and immense physical strength. Oddjob set the standard for future Bond henchmen with his distinctive appearance and deadly skills. His loyalty to Goldfinger is unwavering, and he carries out his master's orders without question. Oddjob's defining moment comes when he uses his steel-brimmed hat to decapitate a statue, demonstrating his lethal precision. His silent demeanor and formidable presence make him a memorable and intimidating adversary for Bond.

Loyalty and Betrayal

Oddjob's loyalty to Goldfinger is absolute, but it ultimately leads to his demise. In the climactic battle at Fort Knox, Oddjob remains steadfast in his mission to protect the bomb, even when it becomes clear that Goldfinger has abandoned him. This unwavering loyalty highlights the henchman's dedication but also underscores the expendability of henchmen in the eyes of their masters.

Case Study: Jaws

Jaws, portrayed by Richard Kiel, is another iconic henchman known for his immense size and steel teeth. Appearing in "The Spy Who Loved Me" and "Moonraker," Jaws is a formidable adversary who remains loyal to his employers despite their villainous intentions.

Loyalty Despite Villainy

Jaws' loyalty is tested throughout his appearances, but he remains committed to his role as a henchman. His loyalty is particularly evident in "Moonraker," where he continues to serve Hugo Drax despite the dangers he faces. Jaws' loyalty is not just a result of fear or coercion; it is also driven by a sense of duty and professionalism.

A Change of Heart

In a surprising twist, Jaws' loyalty shifts in "Moonraker" when he falls in love with Dolly, a fellow captive. This newfound love leads him to question his allegiance to Drax and ultimately join forces with Bond to thwart Drax's plan. This change of heart highlights the complexity of Jaws' character and the potential for redemption, even for a henchman.

Case Study: Nick Nack

Nick Nack, portrayed by Hervé Villechaize, is the diminutive but cunning henchman of Francisco Scaramanga in "The Man with the Golden Gun." Despite his small stature, Nick Nack is a master manipulator who plays a crucial role in Scaramanga's schemes.

Manipulation and Deception

Nick Nack's loyalty to Scaramanga is driven by a combination of fear and ambition. He is promised a substantial inheritance if Scaramanga is killed, which motivates him to manipulate events to his advantage. Nick Nack's ability to deceive and outwit both Scaramanga and Bond makes him a formidable adversary.

Loyalty and Self-Interest

Nick Nack's loyalty is ultimately self-serving. While he appears to be a loyal servant, his true motivation is personal gain. This duality adds depth to his character and highlights the fragile nature of alliances based on self-interest. Nick Nack's eventual capture by Bond underscores the risks of betrayal and the consequences of divided loyalties.

Case Study: Mr. Hinx

Mr. Hinx, portrayed by Dave Bautista, is a modern addition to the roster of Bond henchmen. Appearing in "Spectre," Mr. Hinx is a relentless and physically imposing adversary who serves the criminal organization SPECTRE.

Relentless Pursuit

Mr. Hinx's loyalty to SPECTRE is demonstrated through

his relentless pursuit of Bond. His physical strength and determination make him a formidable opponent, and he stops at nothing to accomplish his mission. Mr. Hinx's loyalty is driven by a sense of duty and a desire to prove himself within the organization.

Loyalty and Ruthlessness

Mr. Hinx's loyalty is characterized by his ruthlessness. He is willing to eliminate anyone who stands in his way, including fellow SPECTRE operatives. This ruthless approach underscores the cutthroat nature of villainous organizations and the high stakes involved in their operations.

Benefits of Being a Henchmen

The relationship between villains and their henchmen offers several benefits, both psychologically and monetarily. Psychologically, henchmen often derive a sense of purpose and belonging from their association with powerful villains. This relationship provides them with a clear role and identity, which can be particularly appealing for individuals seeking validation and recognition. Monetarily, henchmen are often well-compensated for their loyalty and services. They receive financial rewards, luxurious lifestyles, and access to resources that would otherwise be unattainable. These benefits create a strong incentive for henchmen to remain loyal to their masters, despite the inherent risks and moral compromises involved.

Lessons on Loyalty, Trust, and the Fragility of Evil Alliances

The relationships between Bond villains and their henchmen offer several valuable lessons on loyalty, trust, and the fragility of evil alliances:

Loyalty is Often Conditional: The loyalty of henchmen is often driven by self-interest, fear, or ambition. This conditional loyalty can lead to betrayal when personal interests are threatened or better opportunities arise.

Trust is Fragile: The trust between villains and their

henchmen is often tenuous and easily broken. Betrayal is a common theme, as henchmen may turn against their masters to protect themselves or gain personal advantage.

The Cost of Loyalty: Loyalty to a villain comes with significant risks and moral compromises. Henchmen must navigate a dangerous world where their lives are constantly at stake, and their loyalty is often taken for granted.

The Potential for Redemption: Despite their villainous roles, henchmen like Jaws demonstrate the potential for redemption. Personal relationships and moral awakenings can lead to changes in loyalty and actions, highlighting the complexity of human nature.

Conclusion

The role of henchmen in James Bond movies is integral to the franchise's success. Characters like Oddjob, Jaws, Nick Nack, and Mr. Hinx define the archetype of the henchman, each bringing unique traits and dynamics to their relationships with the villains. Through their stories, we learn valuable lessons about loyalty, trust, and the fragility of evil alliances. These henchmen add depth and intrigue to the Bond series, making them unforgettable adversaries for 007.

Chapter 9:

Over The Line: The Consequences Of Obsession For Bond Villains

In the world of James Bond, villains are often driven by powerful obsessions that define their actions and ultimately lead to their downfall. These obsessions, whether for power, control, revenge, or superiority, create complex characters whose motivations go beyond simple villainy. This article explores the role of obsession in Bond villains, examining their psychological profiles, the fine line between passion and obsession, and the broader consequences of their fixations. Through case studies of Max Zorin, Hugo Drax, and Alec "Janus" Trevelyan, we will delve into the dangers of unchecked ambition and the lessons these characters offer.

The Role of Obsession in Villains

Obsession plays a crucial role in shaping the motivations and actions of Bond villains. It drives them to pursue their goals with relentless determination, often at the expense of their humanity and morality. These obsessions are not merely personal quirks but are central to their identities and plans. Whether it is a desire for global domination, revenge, or proving one's superiority, these fixations provide the villains with a sense of purpose and direction. However, this single-minded pursuit often leads to their undoing, as their obsessions blind them to the consequences of their actions and the inevitability of their defeat.

Psychological Sketch of Bond Villains with Obsessive Issues

Bond villains with obsessive tendencies often exhibit traits associated with various psychological disorders, such as narcissistic personality disorder, antisocial personality disorder, and psychopathy. These characters display a pervasive pattern of grandiosity, a need for admiration, and a lack of empathy. They are often manipulative, deceitful, and willing to use violence to achieve their goals.

For example, Max Zorin from "A View to a Kill" exhibits traits of narcissistic personality disorder, with his grandiose sense of self-importance and belief in his superiority. Hugo Drax from "Moonraker" displays obsessive-compulsive tendencies, with his meticulous planning and desire for control over every aspect of his schemes. Alec Trevelyan, also known as Janus, from "GoldenEye," shows signs of antisocial personality disorder, with his disregard for the rights of others and his obsession with revenge.

These psychological profiles highlight the complexity of Bond villains, making them more than just one-dimensional antagonists. Their obsessions are deeply rooted in their personalities, driving their actions and shaping their interactions with Bond and the world around them.

The Fine Line Between Passion and Obsession

Passion and obsession are closely related but distinct concepts. Passion is a strong and intense enthusiasm or desire for something, often leading to positive outcomes and personal fulfillment. It is characterized by a healthy balance between dedication and other aspects of life. In contrast, obsession is an unhealthy fixation on a particular goal or idea, often leading to negative consequences and destructive behavior.

The transition from passion to obsession can be subtle and gradual. Mental illness, such as anxiety disorders, depression, or personality disorders, can exacerbate this shift, causing individuals to lose perspective and become consumed by their ambitions. When passion turns into obsession, it can lead to a loss of control, impaired judgment, and an inability to recognize the harm being caused to oneself and others.

In the case of Bond villains, their obsessions often start as passionate pursuits but eventually consume them, leading to their downfall. This fine line between passion and obsession underscores the importance of maintaining a healthy balance and being aware of the potential dangers of unchecked ambition.

Obsession and Visions of Grandeur

Obsession for a cause can lead to delusions of grandeur, where individuals believe they are destined for greatness or possess extraordinary abilities. This inflated sense of self-importance can result in the dehumanization of entire populations, as the obsessed individual views others as mere obstacles or tools to achieve their grand vision.

For Bond villains, this often manifests in their plans for global domination or mass destruction. Their obsession with their cause blinds them to the value of human life and the ethical implications of their actions. They become detached from reality, believing that their vision justifies any means necessary to achieve it.

Case Study: Max Zorin and His Obsession with Superiority

Max Zorin, portrayed by Christopher Walken in "A View to a Kill," is a prime example of a Bond villain driven by an obsession with superiority. Zorin is a product of a Nazi genetic experiment, which instilled in him a belief in his own superiority and a desire to dominate others. His obsession with proving his superiority leads him to devise a plan to destroy Silicon Valley, thereby monopolizing the microchip market and cementing his dominance in the tech industry.

Zorin's obsession with superiority is evident in his ruthless behavior and lack of empathy. He is willing to sacrifice anyone, including his own employees, to achieve his goals. This single-minded pursuit of dominance ultimately leads to his downfall, as his arrogance blinds him to the risks and consequences of his actions.

Case Study: Hugo Drax and His Obsession with Control

Hugo Drax, portrayed by Michael Lonsdale in "Moonraker," is driven by an obsession with control. Drax is a wealthy industrialist who plans to create a new master race by exterminating humanity and repopulating the Earth with genetically superior individuals. His obsession with control extends to every aspect of his life, from his meticulously planned schemes to his interactions with others.

Drax's obsession with control is rooted in his desire for perfection and his belief in his own superiority. He views himself as a god-like figure, holding the fate of humanity in his hands. This delusion of grandeur leads him to dehumanize others, seeing them as expendable in his quest for a perfect world. Ultimately, Drax's obsession with control leads to his defeat, as his rigid plans are disrupted by Bond's ingenuity and resourcefulness.

Case Study: Alec "Janus" Trevelyan and His Obsession with Revenge

Alec Trevelyan, portrayed by Sean Bean in "GoldenEye," is driven by an obsession with revenge. Once a trusted MI6 agent and Bond's friend, Trevelyan turns against his country and former ally after discovering his parents' betrayal by the British government. Adopting the alias "Janus," Trevelyan seeks to exact revenge on Britain by using a satellite weapon to cause a financial meltdown.

Trevelyan's obsession with revenge consumes him, leading him to betray his country and former comrades. His fixation on avenging his parents' deaths blinds him to the broader consequences of his actions and the collateral damage he causes. This obsession ultimately leads to his downfall, as his personal vendetta against Bond and Britain becomes his undoing.

Lessons on the Dangers of Unchecked Ambition

The stories of Bond villains like Max Zorin, Hugo Drax, and Alec Trevelyan offer valuable lessons on the dangers of unchecked ambition. Their obsessions drive them to pursue their goals with relentless determination, often at the expense of their humanity and morality. These characters serve as cautionary tales, highlighting the potential consequences of allowing ambition to turn into obsession.

Loss of Perspective: Obsession can cause individuals to lose sight of the bigger picture and become fixated on their goals. This narrow focus can lead to poor decision-making and an inability to recognize the harm being caused to oneself and others.

Dehumanization: Obsession with a cause can lead to the dehumanization of others, as individuals view people as mere obstacles or tools to achieve their goals. This detachment from reality can result in unethical behavior and a disregard for human life.

Self-Destruction: The single-minded pursuit of an obsession often leads to self-destruction. Bond villains' obsessions ultimately lead to their downfall, as their fixations blind them to the risks and consequences of their actions.

The Importance of Balance: Maintaining a healthy balance between passion and other aspects of life is crucial. Recognizing the fine line between passion and obsession can help individuals avoid the pitfalls of unchecked ambition and maintain a sense of perspective and empathy.

Conclusion

The consequences of obsession for Bond villains are profound and far-reaching. Characters like Max Zorin, Hugo Drax, and Alec Trevelyan demonstrate how obsession can drive individuals to pursue their goals with relentless determination, often at the expense of their humanity and morality. These villains' stories offer valuable lessons on the dangers of unchecked ambition, the fine line between passion and obsession, and the importance of maintaining a healthy balance in life. By examining the psychological profiles and motivations of these characters, we gain a deeper understanding of the complexities of villainy and the consequences of allowing obsession to consume us.

Chapter 10:

Home Sweet Home: The Coolest Bond Villain Lairs

The James Bond franchise is renowned for its iconic villains and their equally memorable lairs. These hideouts are not just backdrops for the action but are integral to the villains' identities and schemes. From mountaintop retreats to underwater laboratories, Bond villain lairs are a blend of architectural marvels and technological wonders. This article explores the essential elements of a Bond villain lair, the best geographic locations for these hideouts, and reviews some of the most iconic lairs in the series. We will also discuss how to incorporate some of these design elements into our own homes and the cultural significance of these lairs in the Bond films.

Essential Elements of a Bond Villain Lair

A Bond villain lair is more than just a hideout; it is a reflection of the villain's personality, ambitions, and resources. Here are the essential elements that make a Bond villain lair truly iconic:

Secrecy and Isolation: The lair must be hidden from prying eyes, often located in remote or hard-to-reach places. This ensures the villain can operate without interference.

Advanced Technology: Cutting-edge technology is a hallmark of Bond villain lairs. This includes everything from surveillance systems and weaponry to elaborate security measures.

Luxurious Amenities: Despite their nefarious activities, Bond villains enjoy the finer things in life. Their lairs often feature opulent interiors, complete with luxurious furnishings, art collections, and gourmet kitchens.

Strategic Advantage: The location and design of the lair provide a strategic advantage, whether it's a mountaintop offering a bird's-eye view or an underwater base that is difficult to attack.

Thematic Design: The lair's design often reflects the villain's personal theme or obsession, such as a marine biologist's underwater lab or a megalomaniac's space station.

Best Geographic Locations for a Bond Villain Lair

The geographic location of a Bond villain lair is crucial for its secrecy, strategic advantage, and thematic relevance. Here are some of the best locations:

Mountaintops: High-altitude locations offer isolation, a commanding view, and natural defenses. Examples include Blofeld's mountaintop lair in "On Her Majesty's Secret Service".

Islands: Remote islands provide natural isolation and can be fortified easily. Scaramanga's island in "The Man with the Golden Gun" is a prime example.

Underwater: Submerged lairs offer unparalleled secrecy and are difficult to attack. Karl Stromberg's Atlantis in "The Spy Who Loved Me" exemplifies this.

Arctic Regions: The harsh environment provides natural defenses and isolation. Gustav Graves' ice palace in "Die Another Day" is a notable example.

Deserts: Vast, barren landscapes offer isolation and can be easily monitored for intruders. Blofeld's crater base in "Spectre" is a modern example.

Reviews of Iconic Bond Villain Lairs

Piz Gloria (Blofeld's Mountaintop Lair in "On Her Majesty's Secret Service")

Piz Gloria, located atop the Schilthorn in Switzerland, is one of the most iconic Bond villain lairs. This revolving restaurant offers breathtaking panoramic views of the Swiss Alps. In the film, it serves as Blofeld's allergy research institute, accessible only by helicopter. The lair's strategic location and luxurious interiors make it a perfect hideout for a mastermind like Blofeld. Visitors today can enjoy a James Bond brunch and explore the Bond World 007 museum, which features exhibits and memorabilia from the film.

Scaramanga's Island (Phang Nga Bay in "The Man with the Golden Gun")

Scaramanga's island, located in Phang Nga Bay, Thailand, is a stunning natural formation featuring limestone cliffs and hidden coves. The island's remote location and natural beauty make it an ideal hideout for the world's most expensive assassin. The lair includes a solar power plant and a funhouse maze, reflecting Scaramanga's dual interests in renewable energy and deadly games. The island has become a popular tourist destination, known as "James Bond Island," attracting fans from around the world.

Karl Stromberg's Atlantis (The Spy Who Loved Me)

Atlantis, Karl Stromberg's underwater lair, is a marvel of marine architecture. Located off the coast of Sardinia, this giant marine research laboratory is both a scientific facility and a luxurious residence. The lair's submerged location provides secrecy and protection, while its advanced technology and opulent interiors reflect Stromberg's obsession with the ocean. The lair's design includes large windows offering stunning underwater views, a private aquarium, and a dining room that descends into the sea.

Gustav Graves' Ice Palace (Die Another Day)

Gustav Graves' ice palace, located in Iceland, is a striking example of modern architecture and engineering. The palace is constructed entirely of ice and features a grand ballroom, luxurious suites, and a high-tech control center. The lair's Arctic location provides natural defenses and isolation, while its design reflects Graves' cold and calculating personality. The palace's most impressive feature is its ability to withstand extreme temperatures, making it a formidable fortress.

Bond Villain Design Elements to Incorporate into Our Homes

While we may not need a secret lair for world domination, there are several design elements from Bond villain lairs that we can incorporate into our own homes:

Panoramic Views: Large windows and open spaces can create a sense of grandeur and connection to the surrounding environment. Consider adding floor-to-ceiling windows or a rooftop terrace to enjoy the view.

Luxurious Amenities: Invest in high-quality furnishings, art, and decor to create a luxurious and comfortable living space. A home theater, wine cellar, or spa can add a touch of opulence.

Advanced Technology: Incorporate smart home technology for convenience and security. Automated lighting, climate control, and surveillance systems can enhance your home's functionality and safety.

Thematic Design: Personalize your home with a theme that reflects your interests and passions. Whether it's a nautical theme, a modern minimalist design, or a vintage aesthetic, make your space uniquely yours.

Secrecy and Privacy: Create private spaces within your home where you can relax and unwind. A hidden room, a secluded garden, or a private study can provide a retreat from the outside world.

Cultural Importance of the Lairs in the Bond Films

The lairs of Bond villains are more than just settings for action scenes; they are cultural icons that reflect the themes and values of the Bond franchise. These lairs symbolize the power, wealth, and ambition of the villains, serving as extensions of their personalities and plans. They also highlight the contrast between

Bond and his adversaries, emphasizing Bond's resourcefulness and ingenuity in overcoming seemingly insurmountable obstacles.

The design and location of these lairs often reflect contemporary fears and fascinations, such as the Cold War-era obsession with nuclear bunkers or the modern concern with environmental sustainability. By incorporating cutting-edge technology and luxurious amenities, these lairs also showcase the latest trends in architecture and design.

Moreover, the lairs contribute to the visual and narrative appeal of the Bond films, providing memorable backdrops for the action and drama. They have become iconic symbols of the franchise, inspiring countless imitations and parodies in popular culture.

Conclusion

The coolest Bond villain lairs are a blend of architectural brilliance, technological innovation, and thematic design. From the mountaintop retreat of Piz Gloria to the underwater marvel of Atlantis, these lairs are as memorable as the villains who inhabit them. By examining the essential elements and best locations for these hideouts, we gain a deeper appreciation for the creativity and imagination that goes into creating these iconic settings. Whether you're a Bond fan or simply looking for design inspiration, the lairs of Bond villains offer a fascinating glimpse into the world of luxury, secrecy, and ambition.

Chapter 11:

The Bond Villain Fashion: Killing It With Style

The James Bond franchise is not only known for its suave secret agent but also for its stylish and sophisticated villains. These antagonists are often as well-dressed as Bond himself, if not more so. Their wardrobes are meticulously crafted to reflect their personalities, power, and wealth. This article delves into the essential wardrobe elements a Bond villain must possess, explores the various styles and wardrobes of the villains in the Bond movies, and reviews some of the most iconic villain looks. We will also discuss how to incorporate Bond villain fashion into our own lives and the cultural impact of these fashion styles.

Essential Wardrobe Elements a Bond Villain Must Possess

A Bond villain's wardrobe is a crucial part of their character, often reflecting their personality, status, and the nature of their schemes. Here are the essential elements that make up a Bond villain's wardrobe:

Tailored Suits: A well-fitted suit is a staple in a Bond villain's wardrobe. It exudes power, sophistication, and control. The suits are often custom-made, using the finest fabrics and tailored to perfection.

Distinctive Accessories: Accessories such as cufflinks, watches, and pocket squares add a touch of elegance and individuality. These items are often luxurious and unique, reflecting the villain's wealth and taste.

Signature Colors: Bond villains often have a signature color palette that sets them apart. This could be a preference for dark, muted tones or bold, striking colors that make a statement.

Cultural and Thematic Elements: The wardrobe often incorporates elements that reflect the villain's background or thematic obsession. This could be traditional garments, specific patterns, or unique fabrics.

Functional and Stylish Outerwear: Whether it's a trench coat, a fur-lined jacket, or a tailored overcoat, outerwear is both functional and stylish, often adding to the villain's imposing presence.

Styles and Wardrobes of Bond Villains

The styles and wardrobes of Bond villains are as varied as the characters themselves. Each villain's wardrobe is carefully designed to reflect their unique personality and the nature of their evil schemes.

Emilio Largo (Thunderball): Emilio Largo, played by Adolfo Celi, is one of the best-dressed Bond villains. His wardrobe includes a Casablanca-esque double-breasted ivory dinner jacket, which exudes elegance and sophistication. Largo's 8x3 double-breasted blazer looks particularly regal, making him a worthy adversary to Bond.

Auric Goldfinger (Goldfinger): Auric Goldfinger, portrayed by Gert Fröbe, is known for his obsession with gold, which is reflected in his wardrobe. Goldfinger's clothes are often colored gold or in shades that suggest it, like yellow, cream, and brown. His style is flashy and over-the-top, perfectly matching his larger-than-life personality.

Le Chiffre (Casino Royale): Le Chiffre, played by Mads Mikkelsen, has a more subdued yet luxurious style. His wardrobe includes a black velvet dinner jacket with grosgrain silk facings, a black dress shirt, and a black bow tie. This all-black ensemble emphasizes his secretive and menacing nature while maintaining an air of sophistication.

Dr. Kananga (Live and Let Die): Dr. Kananga, portrayed by Yaphet Kotto, has a bold and vibrant wardrobe that reflects his dual identity as a drug lord and a Caribbean dictator. His outfits include a bright red jacket, a red shirt and white jacket combo, and other colorful ensembles. Kananga's wardrobe is as flamboyant as his personality, making him a memorable villain.

Incorporating Bond Villain Fashion Style into Our Wardrobe

While we may not be plotting world domination, we can still incorporate elements of Bond villain fashion into our own wardrobes. Here are some tips:

Invest in Tailored Suits: A well-fitted suit can make a significant difference in your appearance. Invest in a few high-quality, tailored suits in classic colors like black, navy, and grey.

Choose Distinctive Accessories: Accessories can elevate your outfit and add a touch of individuality. Opt for unique cufflinks, a stylish watch, or a pocket square that complements your suit.

Embrace Signature Colors: Find a color palette that suits you and stick to it. Whether it's bold and vibrant or dark and muted, having a signature color can make your wardrobe more cohesive.

Incorporate Cultural Elements: If you have a cultural background or a particular interest, incorporate elements of it into your wardrobe. This could be through patterns, fabrics, or specific garments.

Choose Stylish Outerwear: A good coat or jacket can complete your look. Choose outerwear that is both functional and stylish, such as a tailored overcoat or a trench coat.

Cultural Impact of the Fashion Styles of Bond Villains

The fashion styles of Bond villains have had a significant cultural impact, influencing fashion trends and popular culture. These villains are often seen as style icons, with their distinctive wardrobes becoming a part of their legacy. The meticulous attention to detail in their clothing reflects their personalities and adds depth to their characters.

The fashion styles of Bond villains also highlight the contrast between good and evil, with the villains often dressed in darker, more dramatic clothing compared to Bond's classic and understated style. This visual contrast enhances the storytelling and adds to the overall aesthetic of the films.

Moreover, the fashion styles of Bond villains have inspired designers and fashion enthusiasts around the world. The luxurious fabrics, bold colors, and unique accessories seen in the villains' wardrobes have become a source of inspiration for many, leading to the incorporation of these elements into mainstream fashion.

Conclusion

The wardrobes of Bond villains are a crucial part of their characters, reflecting their personalities, power, and wealth. From Emilio Largo's elegant ivory dinner jacket to Auric Goldfinger's flashy gold ensembles, each villain's wardrobe is meticulously crafted to make a statement. By incorporating elements of Bond villain fashion into our own lives, we can add a touch of sophistication and individuality to our wardrobes. The cultural impact of these fashion styles is undeniable, influencing trends and inspiring fashion enthusiasts around the world. Whether you're a fan of the Bond franchise or simply appreciate good fashion, the wardrobes of Bond villains offer a fascinating glimpse into the world of style and sophistication.

Chapter 12:

Cultural Reflections: How The James Bond Villains Reflect Society

The James Bond franchise has captivated audiences for decades, not only with its suave secret agent but also with its memorable villains. These antagonists are more than just obstacles for Bond to overcome; they are reflections of the societal fears and issues of their times. This article explores how Bond villains mirror societal anxieties, provides case studies on the cultural context of various villains through the decades, and discusses the lessons we can learn about societal values through villainy.

How Bond Villains Reflect Societal Fears and Issues

Bond villains are often embodiments of the fears and anxieties prevalent in society at the time of their creation. These characters serve as a mirror, reflecting the issues that dominate public consciousness. For instance, during the Cold War, many Bond villains were Soviet agents or had ties to the Eastern Bloc, reflecting the West's fear of communist expansion and nuclear annihilation. In more recent films, villains have been depicted as terrorists, corrupt businessmen, or cybercriminals, mirroring contemporary concerns about global terrorism, corporate malfeasance, and digital security.

The portrayal of these villains taps into the collective psyche, making the threats they represent feel more immediate and real. By confronting these fears through the lens of a Bond film, audiences can engage with and process these anxieties in a controlled and entertaining environment. This dynamic not only makes the films more relevant but also allows them to comment on and critique the societal issues of their time.

Case Studies: The Cultural Context of Various Villains Through Decades

Dr. No (1962)

Dr. Julius No, the first major Bond villain, reflects the early 1960s' fear of nuclear technology and the Cold War. His plan to disrupt American missile tests using a nuclear-powered radio beam taps into the anxieties surrounding nuclear proliferation and the potential for global catastrophe. Dr. No's character, with his bionic metal hands, also embodies the era's fascination with and fear of technological advancements.

Goldfinger (1964)

Auric Goldfinger, the titular villain of "Goldfinger," represents the greed and corruption associated with the post-war economic boom. His obsession with gold and his plan to irradiate the United States' gold reserves to increase the value of his own holdings reflect concerns about economic stability and the corrupting influence of wealth. Goldfinger's character is a critique of unchecked capitalism and the moral decay it can bring.

Blofeld (1960s-1970s)

Ernst Stavro Blofeld, the head of the criminal organization SPECTRE, is a recurring villain who embodies the fear of global conspiracies and shadowy organizations. During the 1960s and 1970s, when distrust in government and institutions was high, Blofeld's character tapped into the parancia about secret societies and their potential to manipulate world events. His various schemes, from biological warfare to space-based weapons, reflect the era's anxieties about technological advancements and their potential misuse.

Le Chiffre (2006)

Le Chiffre, the villain in "Casino Royale," reflects the post-9/11 world and the fear of terrorism and financial instability. As a banker to terrorist organizations, Le Chiffre's character highlights the interconnectedness of global finance and terrorism. His plan to win back lost money through a high-stakes poker game mirrors the high-risk financial maneuvers that contributed to the global financial crisis. Le Chiffre's character is a commentary on the dangers of financial speculation and the dark underbelly of global finance.

Silva (2012)

Raoul Silva, the antagonist in "Skyfall," represents the fear of cyberterrorism and the vulnerability of digital infrastructure. As a former MI6 agent turned rogue hacker, Silva's character embodies the threat of insider attacks and the potential for digital sabotage. His personal vendetta against M and his use of technology to wreak havoc reflect contemporary concerns about data security and the power of cybercriminals. Silva's character is a critique of the overreliance on technology and the potential consequences of its misuse.

Lessons on Understanding Societal Values Through Villainy

The portrayal of Bond villains offers valuable insights into societal values and concerns. By examining these characters and their motivations, we can gain a deeper understanding of the issues that have shaped public consciousness over the decades. Here are some lessons we can learn:

Fear as a Reflection of Society: The fears embodied by Bond villains are a direct reflection of the anxieties prevalent in society at the time. By understanding these fears, we can gain insight into the historical and cultural context of different eras.

Critique of Power and Corruption: Many Bond villains represent the corrupting influence of power and wealth. Their schemes often involve exploiting or manipulating systems for personal gain, highlighting the dangers of unchecked ambition and moral decay.

Technological Anxiety: The evolution of Bond villains reflects society's changing relationship with technology. From nuclear weapons to cyberterrorism, these characters embody the fears and uncertainties associated with technological advancements and their potential misuse.

Globalization and Interconnectedness: The global nature of many Bond villains' schemes reflects the increasing interconnectedness of the world. Issues such as terrorism, financial instability, and cybercrime are portrayed as global threats, highlighting the need for international cooperation and vigilance.

Moral Ambiguity: Bond villains often operate in morally ambiguous spaces, challenging the clear-cut distinction between good and evil. This complexity reflects the nuanced nature of real-world issues and the difficulty of finding simple solutions to complex problems.

Conclusion

The villains of the James Bond franchise are more than just adversaries for the iconic spy; they are cultural reflections of the fears, anxieties, and issues that have shaped society over the decades. From the Cold War paranoia of Dr. No to the cyberterrorism fears embodied by Silva, these characters offer valuable insights into the societal values and concerns of their times. By examining the cultural context of Bond villains, we can gain a deeper understanding of the historical and cultural forces that have shaped our world and continue to influence it today.

Chapter 13:

Redemption Of The Bond Villain:
Can A Psychopath Change?

The James Bond franchise has long been celebrated for its thrilling action sequences, charismatic protagonist, and, perhaps most intriguingly, its complex villains. These antagonists often embody the darker aspects of human nature, raising questions about morality, redemption, and the potential for change. This article explores the concept of redemption for Bond villains, particularly those with psychopathic traits, and examines whether true change is possible. We will delve into the evidence (or lack thereof) regarding the ability of psychopaths to change, the inevitability of villains in society, the potential for self-reflection among Bond villains, and provide case studies of villains and henchmen who experienced a change of heart. Additionally, we will compare James Bond to his adversaries and discuss the lessons of good over evil in the Bond movies.

No Evidence Psychopaths Can Change

Psychopathy is a personality disorder characterized by traits such as superficial charm, manipulativeness, lack of empathy, and antisocial behavior. Research consistently shows that psychopaths are resistant to change. Studies indicate that psychopaths do not mellow with age and that their behavior often worsens over time. Attempts to rehabilitate psychopaths have largely been unsuccessful, as their lack of empathy and remorse makes it difficult for them to engage in meaningful self-reflection or change their behavior. This suggests that the redemption of a true psychopath, such as many Bond villains, is unlikely.

We Will Always Have Villains

Villains are an inevitable part of human society. Throughout history, there have always been individuals who exploit, manipulate, and harm others for personal gain. These individuals often embody the fears and anxieties of their time, serving as a reflection of societal issues. In the context of the James Bond franchise, villains represent the ever-present threats to global security and stability. Whether driven by greed, power, or ideology, these antagonists remind us that the battle between good and evil is a constant and ongoing struggle.

The Potential for Self-Reflection of Bond Villains

While true psychopaths may be resistant to change, not all Bond villains fit this mold. Some villains and henchmen in the franchise exhibit moments of self-reflection and moral ambiguity. These characters often have complex motivations and backstories that make them more than just one-dimensional antagonists. For instance, Raoul Silva in "Skyfall" is driven by a personal vendetta against M, stemming from feelings of betrayal and abandonment. This depth adds layers to his character, suggesting that even villains can possess the capacity for self-reflection, albeit limited.

Case Studies: Bond Villains and Henchmen
Who Had a Change of Heart

Jaws (The Spy Who Loved Me, Moonraker)

Jaws, the towering henchman with metal teeth, is one of the most iconic Bond villains. Initially, he is a ruthless killer working for Karl Stromberg and later Hugo Drax. However, in "Moonraker," Jaws undergoes a significant transformation. After meeting and falling in love with Dolly, he begins to question his loyalty to Drax. Ultimately, Jaws turns against Drax and helps Bond save the day. This change of heart highlights the potential for redemption, even among the most fearsome villains.

Alec Trevelyan (GoldenEye)

Alec Trevelyan, also known as Agent 006, starts as Bond's ally but later becomes his adversary. Driven by a desire for revenge against the British government, Trevelyan's motivations are deeply personal. Despite his betrayal, there are moments in "GoldenEye" where Trevelyan's camaraderie with Bond resurfaces, suggesting a lingering sense of loyalty and regret. While he ultimately remains a villain, these moments of vulnerability add complexity to his character.

How James Bond Differs from the Villains

James Bond, the quintessential hero, stands in stark contrast to the villains he faces. Bond embodies the values of loyalty, duty, and justice. While he operates in a morally gray world, his actions are guided by a sense of responsibility and a commitment to protecting the greater good. In contrast, Bond villains are often driven by selfish desires, whether for power, wealth, or revenge. This fundamental difference in motivation sets Bond apart and underscores his role as a force for good in a world fraught with danger and corruption.

Lessons of Good Over Evil in the James Bond Movies

The James Bond franchise consistently reinforces the theme of good triumphing over evil. Bond's victories over his adversaries serve as a reminder that, despite the presence of malevolence in the world, justice and righteousness can prevail. These stories highlight the importance of courage, integrity, and perseverance in the face of adversity. Bond's unwavering commitment to his mission and his ability to overcome seemingly insurmountable odds inspire audiences to believe in the power of good. In a world where villains are a constant threat, characters like James Bond remind us of the need for heroes who are willing to stand up for what is right and make the world a better place.

Conclusion

The redemption of Bond villains, particularly those with psychopathic traits, is a complex and often unlikely prospect. While true psychopaths are resistant to change, the James Bond franchise offers glimpses of self-reflection and redemption among its antagonists. These moments add depth to the characters and highlight the nuanced nature of villainy. Ultimately, the enduring appeal of the Bond series lies in its portrayal of the timeless struggle between good and evil. Through the lens of these thrilling adventures, we are reminded of the importance of heroes like James Bond in maintaining justice and order in an ever-changing world.

Final Thoughts:

What We Can Learn From James Bond Villains

The James Bond franchise has given us some of the most memorable villains in cinematic history. These antagonists are not just obstacles for Bond to overcome; they are complex characters that reflect societal fears, ethical dilemmas, and the darker aspects of human nature. By examining these villains, we can gain valuable insights into the human condition, the nature of evil, and the importance of moral integrity. This article recaps the lessons learned from Bond villains, discusses the significance of understanding villains in personal and societal contexts, and offers final thoughts on the balance between good and evil.

Recapping Lessons Learned from Bond Villains

Throughout the James Bond series, we encounter villains who embody various traits and motivations that offer important lessons. These characters often reflect the fears and anxieties of their times, serving as a mirror to societal issues. For instance, villains like Dr. No and Ernst Stavro Blofeld represent Cold War paranoia and the fear of nuclear annihilation. Characters like Auric Goldfinger and Le Chiffre highlight the dangers of unchecked greed and financial corruption. More recent villains, such as Raoul Silva, reflect contemporary concerns about cyberterrorism and the vulnerability of digital infrastructure. By studying these villains, we learn about the consequences of power, the corrupting influence of wealth, and the ethical dilemmas posed by technological advancements.

The Significance of Understanding Villains in Personal and Societal Contexts

Understanding villains is crucial not only for appreciating their role in storytelling but also for gaining insights into human behavior and societal dynamics. Villains often represent the darker aspects of human nature, such as ambition, greed, and the desire for power. By examining their motivations and actions, we can better understand the factors that drive individuals to commit harmful acts. This understanding can help us recognize and address similar tendencies within ourselves and our society. Moreover, studying villains can foster empathy and a deeper comprehension of the complexities of human behavior. It reminds us that people are not simply good or evil but are shaped by their experiences, choices, and circumstances.

Final Thoughts on the Balance Between Good and Evil

The James Bond franchise consistently explores the theme of the balance between good and evil. Bond, as the quintessential hero, represents the values of loyalty, duty, and justice. His adversaries, on the other hand, embody the darker aspects of human nature and the threats to global security and stability. These dynamic highlights the ongoing struggle between good and evil, emphasizing that the battle is never truly over. The presence of villains serves as a reminder that evil exists and must be confronted. However, it also underscores the importance of heroes like Bond, who are willing to stand up for what is right and protect the greater good. In a world where the lines between good and evil are often blurred, the Bond films remind us of the necessity of moral integrity and the enduring power of justice.

Conclusion

The villains of the James Bond franchise offer valuable lessons about the nature of evil, the complexities of human behavior, and the importance of moral integrity. By examining these characters, we gain insights into societal fears, ethical dilemmas, and the darker aspects of human nature. Understanding villains helps us recognize and address similar tendencies within ourselves and our society, fostering empathy and a deeper comprehension of human behavior. Ultimately, the Bond films remind us of the ongoing struggle between good and evil and the necessity of heroes who are willing to stand up for what is right. In a world fraught with danger and corruption, characters like James Bond inspire us to believe in the power of justice and the enduring triumph of good over evil.